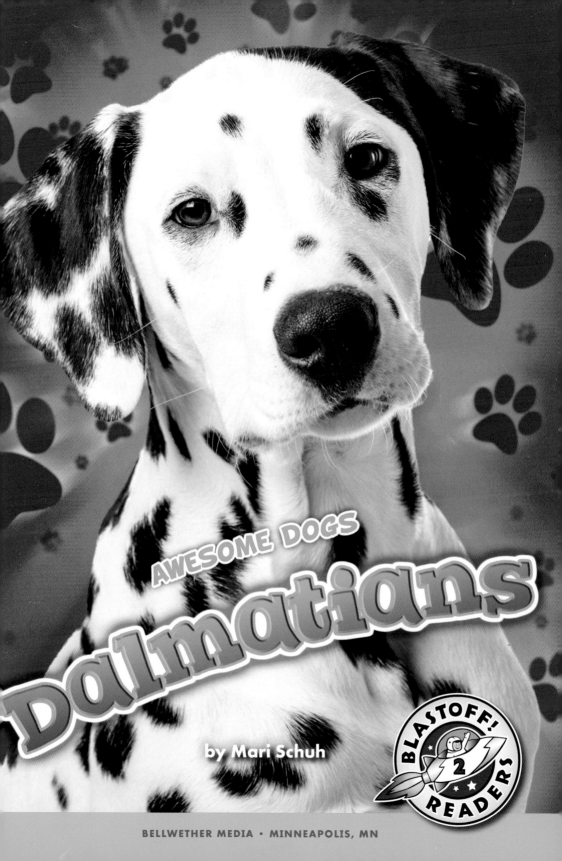

AWESOME DOGS

Dalmatians

by Mari Schuh

BLASTOFF! READERS 2

BELLWETHER MEDIA • MINNEAPOLIS, MN

Note to Librarians, Teachers, and Parents:

Blastoff! Readers are carefully developed by literacy experts and combine standards-based content with developmentally appropriate text.

Level 1 provides the most support through repetition of high-frequency words, light text, predictable sentence patterns, and strong visual support.

Level 2 offers early readers a bit more challenge through varied simple sentences, increased text load, and less repetition of high-frequency words.

Level 3 advances early-fluent readers toward fluency through increased text and concept load, less reliance on visuals, longer sentences, and more literary language.

Level 4 builds reading stamina by providing more text per page, increased use of punctuation, greater variation in sentence patterns, and increasingly challenging vocabulary.

Level 5 encourages children to move from "learning to read" to "reading to learn" by providing even more text, varied writing styles, and less familiar topics.

Whichever book is right for your reader, Blastoff! Readers are the perfect books to build confidence and encourage a love of reading that will last a lifetime!

This edition first published in 2018 by Bellwether Media, Inc.

No part of this publication may be reproduced in whole or in part without written permission of the publisher. For information regarding permission, write to Bellwether Media, Inc., Attention: Permissions Department, 5357 Penn Avenue South, Minneapolis, MN 55419.

Library of Congress Cataloging-in-Publication Data
Names: Schuh, Mari C., 1975– author
Title: Dalmatians / by Mari Schuh.
Description: Minneapolis, MN : Bellwether Media, Inc., [2018] | Series: Blastoff! Readers: Awesome Dogs |
    Audience: Age 5-8. | Audience: K to grade 3. | Includes bibliographical references and index.
Identifiers: LCCN 2016059013 (print) | LCCN 2017005262 (ebook) | ISBN 9781626176133 (hardcover :
    alk. paper) | ISBN 9781681033433 (ebook)
Subjects: LCSH: Dalmatian dog–Juvenile literature.
Classification: LCC SF429.D3 S368 2018 (print) | LCC SF429.D3 (ebook) | DDC 636.72–dc23
LC record available at https://lccn.loc.gov/2016059013

Editor: Betsy Rathburn   Designer: Kathy Petelinsek

Printed in the United States of America, North Mankato, MN.

Table of Contents

Dalmatians are strong dogs known for their **striking** looks.

This medium-sized **breed** is covered in spots!

Dalmatians are part of the **Non-Sporting Group** of the **American Kennel Club**.

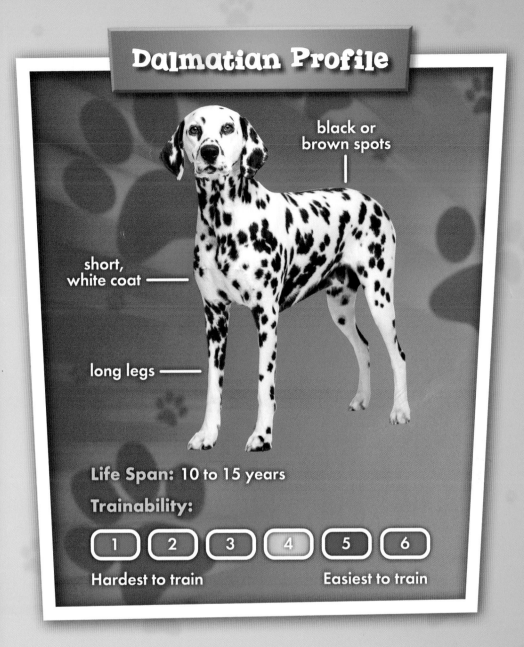

Dalmatian Profile

black or
brown spots

short,
white coat

long legs

Life Span: 10 to 15 years

Trainability:

| 1 | 2 | 3 | 4 | 5 | 6 |

Hardest to train   Easiest to train

Their bodies are covered in short, white fur. Their **coats** have dark spots.

Dalmatians are born all white.
They do not have any spots!

Dalmatian Coats

black
spots

brown
spots

As the puppies grow, black
or brown spots appear on
their coats.

History of Dalmatians

Many believe Dalmatians were named after Dalmatia, a part of Croatia.

Croatia

N
W   E
S

Others think the dogs were named
after a robe some **priests** wear.
No one knows for sure.

Dalmatians have had many jobs. In the past, they worked as circus dogs.

circus dogs

coach dog

They also worked as **coach dogs**.
They ran next to **carriages** to
keep travelers safe.

Dalmatians helped firefighters, too. They cleared paths so fire carriages could get to fires quickly.

Dalmatians are still **mascots** for firehouses today.

Alert and Full of Energy

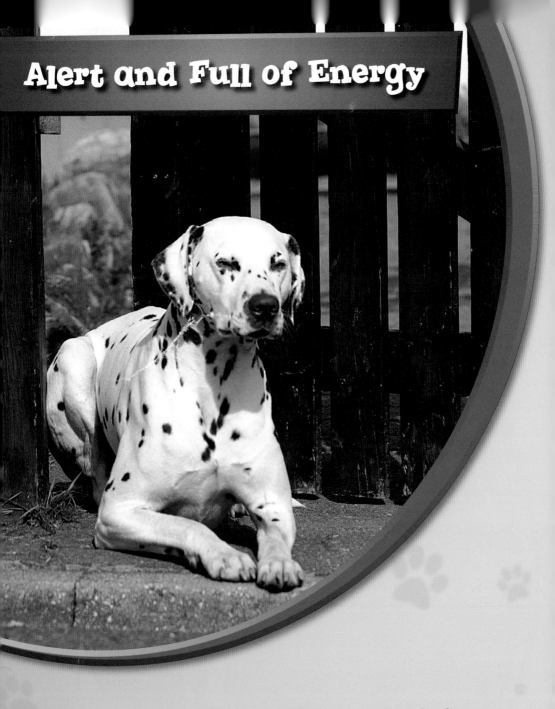

Dalmatians are **alert** watchdogs.
They want to protect their families.

Some Dalmatians bark when they see strangers.

These popular dogs have energy that lasts and lasts. They need a lot of exercise.

Dalmatians are good pets for runners and hikers.

Dalmatians are smart and want to please people. They easily learn tricks.

These **loyal** dogs enjoy being around their families. They often look like they are smiling!

Glossary

alert—quick to notice or act

American Kennel Club—an organization that keeps track of dog breeds in the United States

breed—a type of dog

carriages—large, wheeled vehicles that are used to carry people; most carriages are pulled by horses.

coach dogs—dogs that run next to horse-drawn carriages

coats—the hair or fur covering some animals

loyal—having constant support for someone

mascots—animals or people used as symbols by a group or team

Non-Sporting Group—a group of dog breeds that do not usually hunt or work

priests—people who lead religious ceremonies

striking—beautiful or unusual in a way that calls for attention

To Learn More

AT THE LIBRARY
Bozzo, Linda. *I Like Dalmatians!* New York, N.Y.:
Enslow Publishing, 2017.

Gagne, Tammy. *Bulldogs, Poodles, Dalmatians, and Other Non-Sporting Dogs.* North Mankato, Minn.:
Capstone Press, 2017.

Mathea, Heidi. *Dalmatians.* Edina, Minn.: ABDO
Pub. Co., 2011.

ON THE WEB
Learning more about Dalmatians
is as easy as 1, 2, 3.

1. Go to www.factsurfer.com.

2. Enter "Dalmatians" into the search box.

3. Click the "Surf" button and you will see a
   list of related web sites.

With factsurfer.com, finding more information
is just a click away.

Index

The images in this book are reproduced through the courtesy of: MirasWonderland, front cover; anetapics, p. 4; Maja H., p. 5; otsphoto, p. 6; Eric Isselee, pp. 7, 9, 10; Dora Zett, pp. 8-9; Ron Kimball/ KimballStock, p. 11; Peter Bischoff/ Stringer/ Getty Images, p. 12; Tom Martyn/ Alamy, pp. 12-13; Kathi Lamm/ Exactostock-1491/ SuperStock, p. 14; Minden Pictures/ SuperStock, p. 15; Tierfotoagentur/ Alamy, p. 16; Anna Goroshnikova, p. 17; Grigorita Ko, p. 18; Robin Palmer/ Alamy, p. 19; Everita Pane, p. 20; Aflo Co., Ltd./ Alamy, p. 21.